A Rookie reader®

I Need You

Written by Patricia J. Murphy

Illustrated by Laura J. Bryant

Children's Press®
A Division of Scholastic Inc.
New York • Toronto • London • Auckland • Sydney
Mexico City • New Delhi • Hong Kong
Danbury, Connecticut

To my family, I need you!
-P.J.M.

To Jonathan and Nicole, because everyone needs friends
-L.J.B.

Reading Consultants

Linda Cornwell
Literacy Specialist

Katharine A. Kane
Education Consultant
(Retired, San Diego County Office of Education
and San Diego State University)

Library of Congress Cataloging-in-Publication Data
Murphy, Patricia J., 1963-
    I need you / written by Patricia J. Murphy ; illustrated
by Laura J. Bryant.
        p. cm. — (Rookie reader)
Summary: Illustrations and rhyming text describe things that complement
each other, such as a soup and a spoon, a song and a tune, flowers and a
vase, and a smile and a face.
    ISBN 0-516-22595-2 (lib. bdg.)   0-516-26966-6 (pbk.)
    [1. Stories in rhyme.] I. Bryant, Laura J., ill. II. Title. III. Series.
    PZ8.3.M9257 Iae 2003
    [E]—dc21   2002008782

CHILDREN'S PRESS, AND A ROOKIE READER®, and associated logos are
trademarks and or registered trademarks of Grolier Publishing Co., Inc.
SCHOLASTIC and associated logos are trademarks and or registered
trademarks of Scholastic Inc.
1 2 3 4 5 6 7 8 9 10 R 12 11 10 09 08 07 06 05 04 03

I need you like...

soup needs a spoon.

5

A song needs a tune.

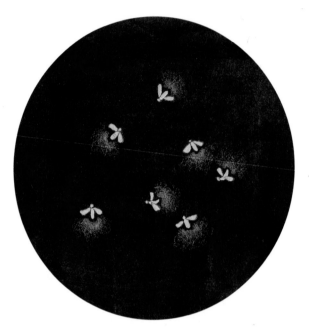

A firefly needs night.
A pillow needs a fight.

9

A button needs a hole.

A flag needs a pole.

I need you like
flowers need a vase.
A smile needs a face.

A snowman needs the cold.
A hand needs a hold.

Mittens need yarn.
A cow needs a barn.

17

18

I need you like
shoes need feet.
A car needs a street.

Birds need nests.
Birthday parties need guests.

21

A gift needs a box.
Artists need smocks.

I need you like
seeds need sun.

A hot dog needs a bun.

An egg needs a hen.
A bear needs a den.

A story needs an end.

The end.

31

Word List (56 words)

a	dog	hole	smile
an	egg	hot	smocks
artists	end	I	snowman
barn	face	like	song
bear	feet	mittens	soup
birds	fight	need	spoon
birthday	firefly	needs	story
box	flag	nests	street
bun	flowers	night	sun
button	gift	parties	the
car	guests	pillow	tune
cold	hand	pole	vase
cow	hen	seeds	yarn
den	hold	shoes	you

About the Author

Patricia J. Murphy writes children's storybooks, nonfiction, early readers, and poetry. She also writes for magazines, corporations, educational publishing companies, and museums. She resides in Northbrook, Illinois. When she is not writing, she *needs* to read, snap photos, do yoga, eat chocolate chip cookies, and spend time with her family.

About the Illustrator

Laura J. Bryant was born and raised in South Florida, where the alligators roam and pink flamingoes flock. She attended the Maryland Institute of Art in Baltimore, Maryland. Laura currently lives in the Shenandoah Mountains of West Virginia with her loving husband, Joshua.